STEPS TO MASTER YOUR EMOTIONS

A Practical Guide to control your mind and emotion fast

Nikki harry

TABLE OF CONTNT

Understanding Self-Love

If you're having a bad day, call a close friend or relative.

If you like fashion, stick to the looks that suit you the most.

To help you get started, consider the ideas listed below:

CHAPTER   FOUR

Strategies to achieve greater success in their lives

What do you consider to be success?

Be devoted goals.

Take notes about your journey.

Enjoy yourself as you go.

Positive thinking is the key

Modify your way of thinking

Be truthful to yourself.

Remove anything that can be a distraction.

Trust yourself

Keep making plans

Avoid being exhausted

CHAPTER FIVE

Things you have to let go of if you rely want to succeed

Quit your unhealthy way of life.

Throw out your short-term thinking.

Stop planning small

Stop making excuses.

Get rid of your fixed mindset

INTRODUCTION

Do you often find yourself overwhelmed with emotions? Do you want to control your mind and emotions so that you can be in a better mental state? In this book, we'll be looking at some simple tricks to help you master your emotions, and gain control over your mind and emotions. So if you're looking for ways to feel better in the moment, or take back power over your thoughts and feelings, keep reading!

TRICKS TO HELP YOU MASTER YOUR EMOTIONS

The greatest moment to deal with a feeling is right when you start to feel and experience it fully. This will prevent it from reappearing repeatedly. You can control your emotions and take charge of your life by adhering to these six simple steps.

LISTEN TO YOUR FEELINGS AND IDENTIFY THEM

Finding out what your feelings are is the first step in learning to control your emotions. To make that move toward emotional control, ponder the following questions.

- What am I actually feeling at the moment?
- Is this how I actually feel?
- Is it something different?

2. Recognize and value your feelings, knowing that they are there to support you.

Emotional mastery is not defined as not repressing or ignoring your emotions. Instead, learning to manage your emotions requires valuing them as an essential aspect of who you are.

Never try to rationalize away your feelings. The notion that anything you feel is "bad" is a powerful tool for stifling open dialogue with both oneself and others.

3. ASK YOURSELF WHAT MESSAGE THIS EMOTION IS TRYING TO TELL YOU.

Having emotional control entails engaging your emotions with inquiry. Your feelings have a lot to say about who you are if you allow them. Curiosity aids you in:

- Break the emotional pattern you're in.
- Conquer the obstacle.
- Ensure the setback doesn't arise again.

4. BE SELF ASSURED

Remembering a period when you felt a comparable emotion and managed it well is the quickest and most effective way to gain emotional control over any mood. You can definitely handle the emotion today since you were able to control it in the past.

5. AIM TO BE SURE

Not only today, but also in the future, you are capable of handling this.

By practicing addressing circumstances where this emotion can surface in the future, you can gain confidence and learn to control your emotions. You can hear, see, and feel how you are managing the event. You will develop the "muscle" necessary to successfully manage your emotions by doing this, which is akin to lifting emotional weights.

6. BE EXCITED AND ACT NOW

Now that you've mastered controlling your emotions, it's time to revel in your ability to:

- Easily manage this feeling.
- Do something straight away.
- Demonstrate that you can handle it.

One of the most effective abilities you can develop is emotional mastery if you want to have a genuine and satisfying life. Tony Robbins' Ultimate Edge, your tool for becoming the best version of yourself, will help you get the encouragement you need to take control of your emotions.

CHAPTER ONE

The Power of Positive Emotions

Every Emotion Is Natural Imagine that you begin to make a list of every feeling you have ever felt. Try it out right away for fun. What do you have planned? Most likely, you listed emotions like joy, sorrow, excitement, anger, fear, gratitude, pride, fear, confusion, stress, relaxation, and amazement. Then divide your list of feelings into two groups: good emotions and negative emotions.

Being able to experience both pleasant and negative emotions comes naturally to us. Even while we may refer to more challenging emotions as "negative," this does not imply that they are undesirable or that we shouldn't feel them. However, the majority of people undoubtedly prefer to experience happy emotions to negative ones. You probably prefer to be joyful than depressed, or confident than unsure.

What counts is how well-balanced our emotions are—how much of each kind of emotion, whether pleasant or negative, we feel.

How Bad Emotions Can Be Beneficial

Negative feelings alert us to potential dangers or difficulties that we may have to face. For instance, fear can warn us of potential danger. It serves as a warning that we might need to defend ourselves. Anger alerts us to someone treading on our toes, going over the line, or betraying our trust. Anger may be an indication that we need to defend our own interests.

Our attention is drawn in by negative feelings. They aid in focusing our attention on an issue so that we can address it. However, experiencing too many unpleasant emotions might leave us feeling drained, worn out, anxious, or stressed. Problems may appear to be too huge to handle when negative emotions are out of balance.

The longer we linger on bad feelings, the worse they make us feel. Negativity only continues if you concentrate on it.

How Joyful Emotions Benefit Us

Although they counteract bad feelings, positive emotions also have other significant advantages.

Positive emotions have an impact on our brains in ways that improve our awareness, attention, and memory as opposed to narrowing our concentration like negative emotions do. We are able to process more information, keep more concepts in mind at once, and comprehend how various ideas are related to one another because to them.

We are better equipped to learn and develop our talents when pleasant feelings allow us to see new possibilities. Better performance on tasks and tests follows from that.

People who regularly experience pleasant emotions are more likely to be happier, healthier, study more effectively, and get along with others.

Science is assisting in our discovery of the potential value of pleasant emotions. Recent researches on the brain have taught experts a lot. Two results that can assist us in maximizing the benefits of pleasant emotions are as follows:

1. Make positive feelings outweigh negative ones.

It is simpler to face challenging circumstances when we experience more happy emotions than negative ones. Our resilience is increased by joyful feelings (the emotional resources needed for coping). They increase our awareness and help us notice more choices for resolving issues.

According to studies, when people experience at least three times as many good emotions as negative ones, they feel and perform at their best. That is brought on by a phenomenon known as the negativity bias.

The propensity for people to focus more on negative than happy emotions is known as the negativity bias. When you consider it, it makes sense: When we experience negative emotions, we are more likely to become aware of issues that may require our immediate attention. Negative emotion tuning in might be a form of survival.

The negative bias has a drawback, though: It can lead us to believe that a day didn't go well, even though we felt both good and terrible emotions equally that day. To tip the scales and make a day appear fantastic, it requires at least three times as many good emotions.

We may improve our performance, feel better about ourselves, and have less negative feelings by forming routines that promote us to feel more positive emotions. If we already experience a lot of negative emotions like fear, sadness, anger, irritation, or stress, then developing happy emotions is very crucial.

It's not hard to develop a daily habit of optimism. There are only two fundamental steps.

1. Take note of and identify your happy feelings. Just begin by concentrating on your emotions. You can pay attention to your feelings as they arise in the present. Or reflect at the end of the day, noting your feelings under various circumstances. For instance, you might feel pleased when you provide the correct response to a question, happy when your dog pursues you around the yard, or loved when your mother attends your game.

You'll probably need to remind yourself to concentrate on your emotions when you first start doing this. However, it becomes simpler the more you do it, just like any habit.

2. Choose a feeling and do something to amplify it. If you select confidence, what supports that feeling? How can you feel that way more often? Before an exam, you might tell yourself, "Yes, I can! "

Alternately, perhaps you sit up taller and practice
moving confidently down the hallways while exuding
a sense of strength and dominance.

Positive feelings are healthy for you and make you
feel happy. Pay attention to these effective tools and
figure out how to fit them into your daily schedule.
Make time in your day for happiness, enjoyment,
friendship, rest, thankfulness, and kindness. You'll
definitely be happier if you make these things a habit.

CHAPTER TWO

Why Do Emotions Matter and What Are They?

What mood are you in? Are you joyful or depressed?

It's likely that if asked, every one of us could name our current emotional state. What does that mean, though? How do emotions affect our daily lives and where do they come from?

Feelings and Emotions

Emotions and sentiments are remarkably similar for the vast majority of people. As a result of their similar meanings, we would naturally see them as synonyms.

Despite their interdependence, emotions and feelings are two entirely different concepts.

Emotions are produced subconsciously and characterize physiological states. Usually, they are individual physiological reactions to certain internal or external circumstances. Contrarily, feelings are cognitive reflections and thoughts that are prompted by individual emotional experiences. This indicates that while we can experience emotions without experiencing feelings, we simply cannot experience feelings without experiencing sensations.

What fundamental feelings do we have?

As many alleged emotions as there are varied perspectives on them among scholars. The seven primary emotions are, roughly speaking: happiness, surprise, fear, disgust, rage, contempt, and sadness.

On the basis of these, we construct secondary emotions, which can total more than 25. But according to recent University of Glasgow research, there are just four fundamental facial emotions used by humans, not seven. However, categorizing emotions is just one discussion stream in general.

Other researchers analyze emotional reactions using the two well-established orthogonal dimensions of arousal (excitement vs. tranquility) and valence (positivity vs. negativity). Any type of regulation of awareness, attention, and information processing involves arousal, which is the psycho-physiological condition of being awake and responsive to stimuli. However, one cannot assess the quality of an emotion just on the basis of the arousal component. The valence dimension addresses emotions of all types, whether they are positive (joy) or negative (fear).

Where in the brain are the "emotional" areas located?

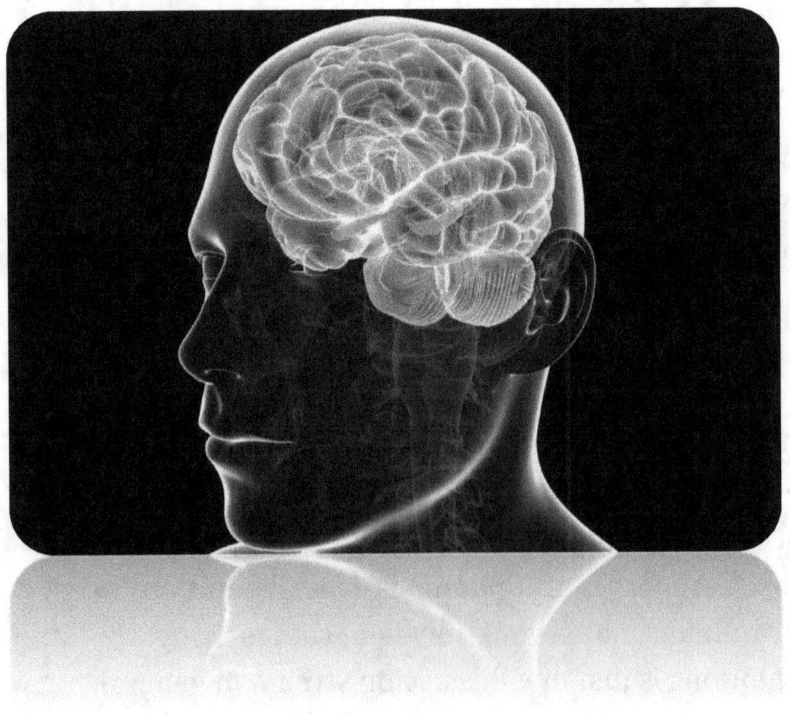

Unfortunately, our good and negative emotions are processed differently throughout different parts of the brain. However, numerous studies have located brain areas that are unmistakably engaged in the processing of both happy and unhappy emotions.

The human brain's neural networks work together to produce emotions These neural networks include self-referential areas in the parietal and occipital regions of the brain, as well as visual and auditory centers in the occipital and temporal regions that analyze incoming information. These regions strongly cooperate with the medial orbit frontal cortex in processing stimuli, such as those that are pleasurable.

Furthermore, research has indicated that when experiencing desire, the nucleus accumbens is engaged. On the other hand, negative emotions like tension, anxiety, and disgust are typically linked to older and deeper brain regions like the insula or the amygdala.

Exactly how unconscious are emotions?
The answer is yes.

In spite of being in a perfectly safe atmosphere and having nothing to be afraid of, you could feel uneasy and frightened when viewing a horror movie at home. You could even attempt to conceal yourself. Stronger breathing, a faster heartbeat, and dilated pupils are all signs that your body is responding.

Your autonomous nerve system has already pulled the triggers and brought about all body changes before you can begin to consciously experience fear or even react with a scream. This demonstrates once further that while sentiments do not always follow from emotions, they do unquestionably influence how we behave.

Do our feelings affect how we think?

Our thinking can be somewhat influenced by our emotions. In short, our initial assessment of a novel scenario is always influenced by our feelings, attitudes, and emotions. Therefore, Ron Richard writes in his article about dispositions, attitudes, and habits, "our emotions are establishing the foundation for the thinking that is to come.

It's actually very beneficial that emotions manifest "pre-cognitively," or before thinking. There is just no time to contemplate when threats are imminent. Instead, emotions "take over" and in a matter of seconds, prompt quick behavioral reactions, preventing undesirable results. Emotions aid in decision-making and provide inspiration for choosing and carrying out the right course of action.

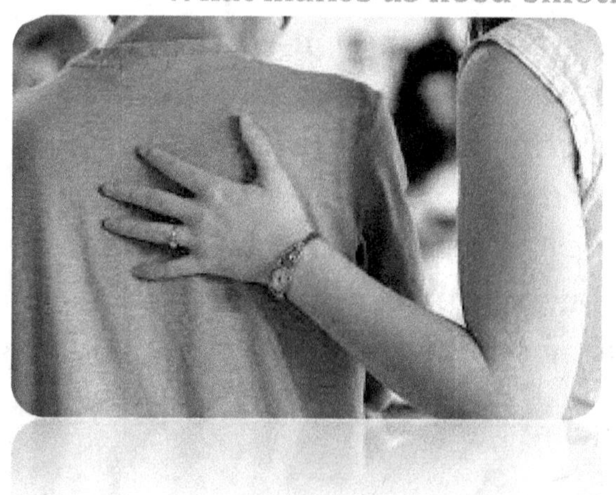

The five primary functions of emotions are eloquently summed up by psychology expert Kendra Cherry as follows: Our ability to act, survive, attack, avoid danger, make judgments, and comprehend others is aided by our emotions. Additionally, they aid in others' understanding of us.

From an evolutionary perspective, brain regions that process cognitive information, like the neocortex, are much more recent than other brain regions that are modulated independently, like the brainstem. Therefore, one could say that the influence of emotions on human behavior is much greater than that of cognition and rational decision-making.

The information that other people's emotions transmit also has an impact on our own. When we interpret someone's facial expression as expressing fear, we have a tendency to scan the area for potentially harmful stimuli. Similar to how we experience safety and comfort when we witness happiness in others. As a result, emotional cues have a simple way of influencing human emotions, cognitions, and behavior.

How are feelings quantified?

There are many different aspects that affect what emotions are and how they are perceived. Since verbal reports appear to be driven by one's knowledge of inner moods, cultural impact, and linguistic skill, questioning people about their feelings may be challenging.

Utilizing physiological measurements, which are universal and more objective than verbal reports, is one approach to get around this. Several cognitive-behavioral techniques, such as EEG, GSR, ECG, facial expression analysis, or eye tracking, can be used to quantify arousal and valence, for example.

CHAPTER THREE

Positive Daily Habits to Boost Your Self-Confidence

Do you radiate confidence when you enter a room? Are you confident in yourself? If not, we are available to support you as you face your fears and pursue your aspirations. You'll learn exactly how to boost your self-confidence so you can rule the world. Let's get started by embracing life and achieving our objectives!

- Concentrate on your advantages and acknowledge your achievements. Never compare your present state to your prior self.
- Talk to yourself kindly and spend time with encouraging individuals.

- By eating healthy, exercising, and getting enough sleep, you can take excellent care of yourself.
- By pursuing your objectives, attempting new things, and overcoming your concerns, you can force yourself to step beyond of your comfort zone.

Describe your advantages. You should concentrate on your strongest areas because everyone is good at something. Keep a list of your accomplishments and cherish your skills. Remind yourself how awesome you are by reading your list of strengths whenever you're feeling low.Think of words like "creative, helpful, smart, intelligent, wonderful dancer" when making your list.

Celebrate your little victories. Understanding your successes will let you realize just how awesome you are. On your path to success, even modest accomplishments matter. Enjoy your accomplishments and the strides you're making toward your objectives for a moment. Take pride in accomplishments like: Finishing a project.

- Baking a fantastic pie
- Achieving a goal's initial step
- Winning a prize at work or school
- Receiving praise for a performance

To combat negative thinking, talk to yourself in a positive way. Everybody has an inner critic, and it may seriously undermine your self-confidence. Fortunately, you have the ability to shift your perspective. Make every effort to exchange your negative thoughts for neutral or good ones.

Use encouraging statements as well to boost your self-worth.

- "I trust in myself,
- "I can succeed if I work hard enough.
- "I am aware of my capacity.
- I'm really pleased with my progress.

Accept compliments with class. When someone compliments you, it usually indicates they think you're outstanding in some way. Don't allow your inner critic discount their complimentary remarks. Reply with a grin and a sincere appreciation of the compliment. It's due to you.

- Say, "I appreciate it very much!" or "Oh, how sweet,"
- Try to congratulate them in return by saying something like, "You look fantastic, too.
- "Adding the compliment to your list of positive qualities about yourself will help you feel more confident.

Never evaluate yourself against others. Because you are unique, you won't be like other people. Furthermore, any comparisons you draw are unfair because you are only viewing a small portion of other people's life. Use your former self as a yardstick for success rather than others. You can then concentrate on building a life that makes you happy.

Remember that the highlights of someone's life are all you see on social media. Usually, you don't notice the terrible days and times when you doubt yourself.

Get a good, encouraging group of individuals around you. Your best traits can be maintained when you have a strong support network. Find the people in your life that make you feel great after spending time with them. Plan to spend time with people who are supportive of you and who make you feel good.

Don't listen to the "should" that your excessively supportive relatives advise you to do. Maintain focus on your objectives.

Give yourself some grace. Give yourself the respect and grace to admit mistakes. Give yourself a break; we're all human. Make an effort to speak to yourself as you would to a close friend. As with everyone else, you are deserving of sympathy.

- The only thing I can do is my absolute best, she said.
- "Mistakes are common to everyone. Everything is fine.
- I will simply view this as a teaching moment. I'll work harder the following time.

Engage in activities you find enjoyable. Having the confidence to follow your passions gives you a sense of individuality and accomplishment. In addition, you deserve time to devote to your happiness. To spend time with friends and to engage in your hobbies set aside time.

- Be creative.
- Attend a culinary class.
- Spend one or two nights a month out with friends.
- Buy brunch Play a sport.
- Launch a band.
- Exercise of Self-Care

Wear whatever makes you feel beautiful. When you're feeling your best, you look your best. Decide to create a wardrobe that makes you happy rather than following trends. You'll look fantastic because of your inner confidence, we promise.

Adopt a balanced diet. Consume plenty of fruits and vegetables for a balanced diet that will help you feel and look your best. Limit your intake of junk food and sweets instead because they are less nutrient-dense.

Your confidence may soar if you're feeling good.

You may have a bowl of oatmeal with apples or bananas in it for breakfast or yogurt with fruit chunks in it.

You might eat a delectable turkey wrap with lettuce, tomato, and a side of tiny carrots for lunch.

You might instead favor a salad that includes a pouch of tuna.

Dinner options include sautéed vegetables with grilled chicken and a baked sweet potato or grilled vegetables with fish served over a bed of rice.

Exercise: You feel more assured and capable when you look after yourself. Spend 30 minutes a day, five days a week, working out for optimal health.

Try something enjoyable, like playing tennis, taking a friend for a stroll, or dancing to your favorite tunes.

So that you won't forget, schedule some exercise throughout your day.

Make working out more enjoyable by inviting a buddy or significant other. You'll also have a partner in accountability that way.

Get enough rest. Experts assert that getting enough rest truly boosts your confidence.

Teenagers require between 8 and 10 hours of sleep per night, while the average adult requires at least 7 hours. Maintain a sleep routine to ensure that you get the rest you require to feel confident.

To make it a habit, try to go to bed and wake up at the same time each day. This will help you fall asleep more easily and wake up feeling rested.

Do some daily meditation. Your confidence will increase if your mind is tranquil because it will make you more self-aware. The practice of meditation also helps you to be nonjudgmental toward your ideas.

Meditating is quite simple, and you can do it anywhere.

Practice being thankful: You can keep in mind how fortunate you are by focusing on all the positive aspects of your life. To help you stay focused on the good things, start keeping a gratitude journal.

Add three things to your list each day at the absolute least. Read over your list to assist yourself get back up when you're having a moment of doubt.

- You might respond, "My closest friends, my loved ones, my cat, nice books, coffee, the sun, etc.
- "Reiterating items from your list is OK. The first three ideas that come to mind should be noted.
- Leaving Your Comfort Zone

Set and work toward sensible objectives. Feeling confident might inspire you to pursue your goals, which are completely within your reach. After deciding on a goal, divide it up into more manageable steps. To construct the life you want, begin working toward your objective right now.

- A goal could be to complete a marathon, sell your artwork, produce a book, or land your ideal job.
- Your self-confidence will rise as you go closer to your objective.

- Possess self-confidence! You have things under control.

Attempt new things: Your horizons will be expanded through new experiences, and you'll come to understand your full potential. Make a list of several activities you want to try, such as 10K running or bungee jumping. After that, go out and enjoy crossing things off your list.

- Attend a class in art.
- Ascend a rock wall.
- Consume Korean barbecue.
- Tell ten strangers "hello.
- "Cook enchiladas.
- • Sleep in a creepy location.
- Bike along a boardwalk or sea wall.

Give up trying to be flawless. Nobody is flawless, so why set that bar for yourself? Set goals for yourself just like you would for a friend. Do the same for yourself as you presumably did for them. You can

only do your absolute best, and it's good if that best
varies from day to day.

Don't expect yourself to be "excellent" at everything
right immediately because everyone begins out as a
beginner. If you continue pushing forward, you'll get
where you're going.

There are times when you simply have to let things
go. Even if your painting, book, or handmade banana
bread isn't "perfect," it's still preferable to share your
works with others rather than keeping them to
yourself.

Recognize opportunities in failure. When you fail at
something, it is quite disappointing. On the path to
success, it is also a crucial step. Even the most
successful people in the world have to deal with
failure. When you fail, learn from the situation and try
again. Finally, it will all be a part of your success
story, and you'll be confident enough to do anything.

Imagine if you registered for a marathon but did not
have enough time to prepare for it. You'll be a better
runner than when you initially started the race if you

give yourself more time to train for it the following time.

Similar to this, you might have auditioned for a play and were given an ensemble part rather than the lead. As a member of the group, you'll gain a lot of knowledge and probably get some comments that you can apply to your next audition.

Face your phobias. It's simple to allow your anxieties prevent you from accomplishing the things that are most important to you. However, as you overcome fear, your confidence soars and it becomes simpler to pursue your passions. Just make the first move toward facing your phobia. You'll find it easier as you gain confidence, we promise.

- You can be shy in front of others.
- Join a debate team, a Toastmasters group, or sign up to read at an open mic.
- Maybe chatting to strangers makes you uncomfortable.

Talk to 5 people you pass every day, such as the
grocery store cashier and the neighbor you see while
out for a walk.

It's possible that you worry that your writing isn't
excellent enough. Attend a writing session and read a
piece you wrote.

Support others. Your self-confidence is boosted by
being a force for good in the world. Do random acts of
kindness and provide a helping hand to make a
positive difference. Volunteer for an organization that
supports a cause that is dear to your heart, such as
feeding the homeless or caring for animals, if you
have the time.

To help others, you don't have to take on a big task.
Sometimes it's enough to just be there for your loved
ones.

CHAPTER FOUR

Everybody has a different definition of success. Success is something that everyone aspires to have, whether it means having a wonderful career, a home, or a family. When you do succeed in achieving your goals, it makes you feel good, increases your incentive to work hard, and demonstrates that you have had an influence in a cutthroat society.

In this post, we'll define what success can include and go through some advice to support you along the way.

Making a list of what success means to you and your family will help you define success for yourself before you ever attempt it. Then, give specific instructions on how to put them into practice in order to succeed.

To enhance your education or pursue professional training, for instance, would be a possible action if your success, as an example, is having a high-paying career. The implementation of daily or weekly writing goals to foster a talent you regard as successful, such as writing, can be a possible course of action.

Depending on how you define success, there are actions you may take to increase your level of success. However, there is no one technique that is necessarily better than another.

Below are tips to help you become successful in life:

You can discover inspiration to succeed if you are dedicated. Make a list that contains your objective, your level of dedication to it, and the steps you are prepared to take to get there.

It's important to remain committed to your plan. It is helpful to set aside at least 15 minutes every day to think about and carry out your plan. This will aid in maintaining your concentration and help you remember your goal.

When evaluating your commitment to your goal, it's imperative to make sure you have appropriate expectations for both the outcome and yourself. If your perseverance doesn't bear fruit after a certain period of time, you should change your goal and take any required steps.

Sometimes it helps to get help from a friend or a family member to make sure you follow through on your commitments. Having someone to point out your shortcomings and celebrate your accomplishments might help you stay focused on your goal.

Take notes about your journey.

Instead of focusing just on the results of your work, take into consideration the minor steps necessary to succeed. If you allow yourself to enjoy small victories along the way, reaching your goal will turn into a new adventure every day. Additionally, you'll be more likely to stay on track. You'll learn interesting new facts along the way if you do this, and it can aid in your personal growth.

Enjoy yourself as you go.

It will be more difficult to succeed if the process of achieving anything gets too arduous. Keep your goals enjoyable and light-hearted to have an emotionally pleasant experience and continue going forward without losing perspective. It could be exciting and pleasant to realize your potential.

Positive thinking is the key

Trusting in yourself and your capacity for success is the key to cultivating a positive outlook. In order to persevere despite difficulties in your way, any negative ideas should be replaced with optimistic ones.

You're probably going to pick up new skills and develop new ways of thinking along the way to success. Your objectives won't be attained right now. It is crucial to approach the process optimistically because they will require practice and dedication to attain.

To improve a difficult circumstance, you might need to alter your perspective while traveling. Instead than focusing on your awful day or week, try to visualize a pleasant one.

Give yourself the chance and the space to think solely positively about your predicament, and then observe how much your day or week transforms. If you persist in doing this, your entire life might be altered.

Be truthful to yourself.

You may need to be really honest with yourself if you discover that your aim has come to a standstill. Once you've gotten to a consensus, work to develop a strategy that will enable you to succeed.

Encourage yourself to push past your comfort zone. This could entail adding another round of squats to your routine, speaking with your boss about a promotion, or even enrolling in a challenging college course you hadn't thought about before.

Make a list of the activities and people in your life that occupy your time or distract you. This may be a phone call, a television program, or even a stressful person in your life. When it's time to concentrate on your goal, turn off your phone and place it in a different room.

Put the remote across the room and turn off the TV. Only stay in touch with those who have a positive influence on your life. The greatest time to begin modifying your behaviors is right now so that you can concentrate on succeeding without being distracted.

Trust yourself

You cannot rely on others to assist you in achieving your objectives. You cannot let your best friend replace you in a class. You cannot receive a promotion from your mother. The assistance of your partner will not help you lose more weight. All of these tasks must be completed by you alone.

Although it may be helpful to rely on others for emotional support, keep in mind that your friends and family may have needs that are distinct from your own. Holding yourself accountable for reaching your goals and prioritizing yourself is essential.

Keep a schedule as you work toward your goals. Create a customized calendar for yourself and write down objectives like, "I will run a mile in seven minutes by the end of the month," or "I will save $5,000."By the end of the year"

Even if you don't accomplish your goal, your calendar will still show where you started and how far you've come. If you plan your goals and keep track of them on a calendar, you will always have proof of your advancement. Possession of something tangible increases perseverance in obtaining success

Though you should strive to avoid being hooked on it, keep your eyes on your goal. If you make the journey fun while still getting things done, you'll stay motivated without exhausting yourself. If you spend all your time contemplating your goal while sitting immobile, you run the risk of burning out.

Your formerly enjoyable task begins to feel more like a burden than something you want to finish. Continue learning about how much you can achieve and improve upon to prevent burnout.

Things you have to let go of if you rely want to succeed

Sometimes, giving up some things is all that is necessary to achieve success and move closer to the person we can become.

Even if every one of us may have a different notion of success, there are some things that are universal and will help

Some of these ou succeed if you give up on them.

You can give up on right now, while others might require a little more time.

Keep your physique in good shape. Your residence there is your sole option.

Everything in life starts here if you want to do anything. Your health comes first, and there are only two considerations you should make in this regard:

1. A nutritious diet

2) Physical Exercise

Take baby steps; one day, you'll be glad you did.

Even though you only have one life, if you live it well, that's all you really need.

Successful people have short-term habits they must develop daily in order to achieve their long-term objectives, which they are aware of.

You should embody these healthy practices rather than just practicing them.

There is a distinction between exercising because it's who you are versus exercising to attain a summer body.

"The world is not served by your settling for less. Shrinkage for the purpose of removing any potential for insecurity in the eyes of others is not enlightened. Like children, everyone of us was created to shine. Everyone of us possesses it; it is not exclusive to any of us. When we let our light shine, we unintentionally give others the go-ahead to do the same. We naturally liberate others when we are free of our own fear.

— Marianne Williamson

Your complete potential can never be realized if you never make an effort to seize excellent possibilities or let your aspirations come true.

What you could have accomplished won't ever be of any use to the world.

Therefore, express your thoughts, don't be frightened of failing, and definitely don't be afraid of succeeding.

It's more important how you play the hand than the cards you're dealt.

Regardless of where they started, their flaws, or their prior mistakes, successful people understand that they are ultimately in charge of their lives.

It is both terrifying and exciting to realize that you are in charge of what occurs in your life going forward.

And once you do, it's the only way you can succeed since we can't advance personally or professionally when we make excuses.

Your life won't be lived for you by anybody else.

Get rid of your fixed mindset

Future ownership will go to those who pick up new talents and combine them in novel ways. People who have a fixed mindset think their intelligence or talents are just fixed traits, and they believe talent alone can bring about success without any other factors. They're in error.

Effective people are aware of this. They devote a significant amount of time each day to cultivating a growth mindset, learning new things, gaining new abilities, and altering their perspectives in order to improve their life.

Never forget that who you are today is not always who you must be tomorrow.

"I'm growing better and better every day in every aspect," you say.

Success appears overnight is a myth.

Successful people understand that daily tiny improvements add up over time and will produce the desired outcomes.

Because of this, you should make plans for the future while concentrating on the day that is right in front of you. Aim to make just 1% progress every day

Perfection is beaten by shipping.

Despite our best efforts, nothing will ever be faultless.

Our inability to act and release our invention into the world is frequently due to our fear of failure (or even success). However, if we wait for everything to be perfect, we risk missing out on a lot of possibilities.

To improve (that 1%), "ship," and then improve.

You won't go anywhere if you stop and throw rocks at every dog that barks. Successful people are aware of this. Because of this, they pick a single object and subdue it. Whether it's a business idea, a chat, or a workout, it doesn't matter.

Being totally focused on one job and present is essential.

We have some influence over some things, but not all of them.

It's crucial to tell these two apart.

Focus on the things you can control and distance yourself from the things you can't. Keep in mind that sometimes the only thing you have control over is how you feel about a situation.

Nobody can be upset while saying "Bubbles," so keep that in mind.

To achieve greatly, one must endure great suffering; to achieve little, one must endure little suffering; to achieve much, one must endure great suffering. Mr. James Allen

Successful people are aware that in order to reach their objectives, they will need to refuse certain requests made by their friends, family, and coworkers.

You could give up some short-term pleasure now, but when your objectives are achieved, it will all have been worthwhile.

Delete the negative folks.

"The five individuals you spend the most time with make up the average of who you are."

Who we are depends on the people we spend the most time with.

People who are more accomplished than us exist as well as others who are less accomplished in both their personal and professional lives. Your success and average will both decline if you spend time with people who are behind you.

But no matter how difficult it may be, spending time with individuals who are more successful than you will help you succeed.

Look around you to determine whether you need to make any adjustments.

"The only guaranteed way to keep people pleased is to do nothing important."

Consider your identity as a market niche.

There will be a sizable number of people who enjoy that specialty and some who don't. And no matter what you try, the market won't accept you as the only option.

No need to defend yourself—this is very normal.

The only thing you can do is be true to yourself, constantly strive to be better and add value, and understand that the increasing number of "haters" is a sign of your success.

The issue is that you still think you have time.

In today's world, impulsive online browsing and television viewing are disorders.

Never let these two serve as a diversion from your objectives or your life.

You should reduce (or perhaps eliminate) your reliance on either unless it is essential to achieving your goals, and instead use that time to activities that will improve your life.

CHAPTER SIX

The Best Way to Take Control of Your Emotions

It's more crucial than you might think to be able to recognize and communicate your emotions.

Your reactions as the felt response to a certain circumstance are significantly influenced by your emotions. When you're tuned in to them, you have access to crucial knowledge that makes possible:

- decision-making
- a successful relationship
- regular
- interactions
- self-care

Even though feelings can be beneficial in day-to-day living, when they feel out of control, they can have a negative impact on your emotional wellbeing and interpersonal connections.

Any emotion, including some you may consider to be pleasant, like ecstasy, joy, or others, can become so intense that it becomes impossible to manage, according to a therapist in Tarzana, California.

You can retake control, though, with a little practice. Having effective emotional management abilities may be related to wellbeing, according to two research from 2010Trusted Source. Additionally, the second study discovered a probable connection between these abilities and financial success, so investing some time in that area could actually pay off.

Think over the following advice to assist you in getting started.

- Examine the effect of your feelings.

- Not all strong emotions are bad.

Emotions, in Botnick's opinion, add energy, uniqueness, and color to our lives. Strong emotions could be a sign that we fully accept life and aren't repressing our basic reactions.

It's very normal to experience moments of emotional overload when something wonderful, tragic, or when you feel like you've missed out occurs.

So how do you see a problem when it happens?

Frequently irrational emotions can result in:

- Conflict in a friendship or relationship
- A problem connecting with others.
- Issues at the office or school.
- a desire to use drugs to help you control your emotions
- Emotional or physical outbursts.

Spend some time evaluating how your irrational emotions are impacting your daily life. Problem regions will be simpler to find as a result (and track your success).

You could be in charge of your emotions with a dial. if it were that easy. But imagine for a moment if you could handle your emotion in this way.

You would not desire to leave them running continuously at maximum efficiency. The same applies to turning them fully off.

When you repress or suppress your emotions, you prevent yourself from experiencing and expressing them. This could happen accidently or on purpose (suppression) (repression).

Both can cause symptoms that indicate physical and mental illness, including:

- Anxiety
- Depression

- Sleep problems.
- Muscular spasms and discomfort
- a problem controlling tension
- Misuse of drugs

When you are learning to control your emotions, make sure you aren't just ignoring your emotions. Healthy emotional expression requires finding a balance between strong emotions and no emotions at all.

Recognize your emotions.

By giving yourself some time to be a sign of on your emotion, you can begin regaining control. Take the example of a few months of dating. They declined the date you tried to set up last week because they claimed to be too busy. I'd like to see you soon, you texted back again yesterday. Could we meet this week?

Over a day later, they finally respond:

"Can't Busy" Suddenly, you're feeling really upset. Without pausing, you fling your phone across the room, tip over your trash can, and kick your desk, spraining your toe.

You can interrupt by inquiring:

- What am I currently feeling? (Disappointed, perplexed, and enraged).
- What took place to give me this feeling? (They dismissed me without providing an explanation.)
- Is there another, more logical explanation for the situation? (Maybe they're dealing with something they don't feel comfortable talking about, like stress, illness, or another problem. They may intend to provide further details when they can.
- In light of these emotion what do I wish for? (Scream, throw things in anger, and send an offensive SMS back.)
- Can you handle things in a more effective way? (Ask if all is well. Question their next availability. Take a stroll or a run.

By refocusing your thoughts and coming up with potential alternatives, you might lessen the impact of your initial, irrational response.

Prior to this response being automatic, considerable time may pass. It will get simpler as you practice running these processes through your thoughts (and more effective).

Accept every emotion you feel.
If you want to get better at managing your emotions, try downplaying them to yourself.

It may seem helpful to tell yourself, "Just calm down," or "It's not that big of a deal, so don't stress out," when you begin to hyperventilate following fantastic news or collapse on the floor sobbing and shouting when you can't find your keys.

However, this discredits your experience. To you, it is really important.

If you accept your feelings as they are, you'll feel more at ease with them. By improving your comfort level with them, you can feel overwhelming emotions more fully and prevent dramatic, counterproductive reactions.

For instance, try:

"I'm not happy because I often lose my keys, which makes me late. I should put a dish on the shelf at the door to remind me to leave them there.

Reliable Source Accepting emotions may lead to greater life happiness and fewer mental health issues. Additionally, believing that emotions are constructive may result in higher levels of happiness. Trusted Source

Maintain a mood diary.

Your sentiments and the reactions they elicit can be written down (or typed out), which can help you identify any problematic tendencies.

Occasionally it's enough to mentally trace your thoughts back through your feelings. You may be able to think about feelings more deeply if you put them in writing.

It as well helps in recognizing the circumstances, including challenges at work or family disputes that result in emotions that are more challenging to control. The creation of more efficient management approaches is made possible by the discovery of specific triggers.

It is most advantageous to journal every day. Keep a journal handy and write down any intense feelings or emotions as they come up. Track your response and the triggers as much as you can. If your response wasn't helpful, use your diary to research further potential solutions that might be.

Breathe deeply.

There is a lot to be said for the power of taking a deep breath, regardless of how crazily happy or angry you are.

Slowing down and paying attention to your breathing won't make the feelings go away on their own (and remember that's not the point).

Nevertheless, using deep breathing techniques can help you to calm down, distance yourself from the intense feeling that was initially present, and prevent any excessive reactions that you'd wish to avoid.

When you next notice that your emotions are taking over:

- Take a deep breath in. The diaphragm, not the chest, is where you take in deep breaths. It could be beneficial to imagine your breath coming from deep within your abdomen.
- Hold on. After counting to three, softly let your air out.
- Consider using a mantra. A mantra like "I am peaceful" or "I am relaxed" may be useful to some people.
- Understanding when to use your voice

Even strong emotions have their proper times and places. For instance, crying uncontrollably when a loved one passes away is a relatively typical reaction. You might be able to release some of your rage and

anxiety after getting dumped by screaming or even
striking your pillow.

Restraint is necessary in other circumstances, though.
Screaming at your manager about an unfair
disciplinary action won't help, no matter how irate
you are.

Knowing when to express your sentiments and when
to hold them for the time being can be learned by
being aware of your surroundings and the scenario.

Take a break for a while.

In order to make sure that you're reacting to
powerful emotions logically, according to Botnick,
you need distance yourself from them.

This distance could be a physical one, such as leaving
a difficult situation. But you can also create some
mental space by changing your focus.

While it's not good to entirely deny or ignore feelings, it is acceptable to put them on hold until you are in a better position to handle them. Just be sure to go back and see them. Diverting yourself in a healthy way is just temporary.

Try:

- Going for a walk
- Viewing a humorous video talking to a close relative
- Spending some time with your animal

If you already engage in regular meditation, it may be one of your go-to strategies for handling strong emotions.

Your ability to be more conscious of all emotions and sensations can be improved through meditation. When you meditate, you're teaching yourself to sit with those emotions, to notice them without criticizing yourself or making an effort to alter or suppress them.

As was already mentioned, learning to accept all of your feelings can make managing your emotions easier. Meditating helps you gain these acceptance skills more. Additional benefits include deeper sleep and more relaxation.

You might start by consulting our overview of the various meditation techniques.

When you're stressed out a lot, it can be difficult to keep your emotions under control. Even people who are usually skilled at controlling their emotions may find it harder to do so under situations of intense stress and tension.

By lowering your stress levels or adopting more efficient stress management skills, you can better manage your emotions.

Stress reduction is also possible through mindfulness practices like meditation. They can lessen it, but they won't make it go away.

Other beneficial techniques for managing stress include:

- Scheduling conversation (and humor) with pals
- Exercise
- Spending time in the out
- Doors allowing
- Time for leisure and interests
- Consult a therapist

It could be time to seek out professional assistance if your emotions are still too much for you to bear.

Emotional dysregulation and mood fluctuations that last for a long time or continue are symptoms of several mental health disorders, such as bipolar disorder and borderline personality disorder. According to Botnick, having trouble controlling your emotions might also be related to trauma, familial problems, or other underlying difficulties.

You can receive empathetic, nonjudgmental support from a therapist while you:

- Investigate the causes of poorly controlled emotions
- Deal with extreme mood swings
- Practice questioning and rephrasing
- Distressing feelings to help you up-regulate limited emotional expression or
- Down-regulate powerful sentiments

Strong emotions and mood swings may trigger unpleasant or harmful notions, which may finally result in helplessness or despair.

Eventually, this cycle may lead to counterproductive coping strategies like self-harm or even suicidal ideation. Please don't hesitate to talk to a loved one if you start to feel the need to hurt yourself or have suicidal thoughts rely on so they can assist you obtain support instantly.

CHAPTER SEVEN

What Emotional Management Skills Are and How to Develop Them

A set of abilities called emotional management can assist you in responding to people or events in a healthy way. Your career will benefit from learning how to control your emotions since it will enable you to make thoughtful decisions and build relationships with people.

Even though it could take some time and work, developing your emotional management abilities might benefit your career.

In this piece, we define emotional management skills, discuss their significance, outline five essential emotional management talents, and offer advice on how to hone your own.

What do you mean by emotional management skill?

Emotional control talents are aptitudes that assist you in controlling your emotional reactions to circumstances. They are an important component of emotional intelligence, a word used to describe a person's capacity to recognize and comprehend their own feelings as well as those of others. The ability to control your emotions can help you become a productive employee and a helpful colleague, albeit it may take some time and work to develop these skills.

Why is it crucial to have emotional management skills?

It may be simpler for professionals who can control their emotions to act logically and make wise professional decisions under high-stress circumstances. Professionals in a variety of fields and professions, including those in leadership, can benefit from learning effective emotional management techniques. You can do a variety of tasks with the aid of emotional management techniques, such as:

- Settling a dispute with clients or coworkers
- Delivering presentations or speaking in front of an audience
- Helping clients
- Leading performance reviews
- Educating new teammates
- Guiding others
- Completing duties within time limitations
- Adapting to alterations in project plans

Five essential techniques for managing emotions skill

The following are some examples of emotional control abilities that can advance your career:

1. **Acceptance**

The capacity to accept your feelings without giving them a value can help you respond to situations that are making you feel a specific way rationally. You can frequently recover from an emotional reaction more quickly and concentrate on the subsequent task by acknowledging your emotions. By connecting your own emotions to those of others, developing emotional acceptance can also aid in the development of empathy.

2. Self-awareness

Understanding your own emotional state gives you the ability to anticipate how a circumstance or person will affect you. This ability is known as self-awareness. It can help you learn how to better respond to events by allowing you to monitor your emotional responses. You can take steps to ensure that you are as prepared as possible for the workday, for instance, if you realize that being prepared helps you feel more at ease and confident at work. Your stress levels can be reduced and your resistance to change or hurdles increased if you feel safe in your work environment.

3. Empathy

Empathy is the capacity to use personal experience to relate to the feelings of others in a given scenario. Empathy can be used in the workplace to foster meaningful connections with coworkers and avoid disputes. Using empathy, you can spot when a coworker needs assistance managing their workload and comprehend their frustration when faced with a challenge or delay. Understanding their emotions will make it easier for you to collaborate with them to find a solution.

4. Reflection

By isolating the emotion from the situation, reflecting enables you to understand why you felt the way you did in response to a scenario or person. Furthermore, it might help you solve issues. For instance, it could be helpful to consider whether you disagree with the decision your coworker made or whether it makes you feel insecure that you weren't present for the discussion if you had a disagreement with them about one they made while you were away at work. Understanding the root of your emotions might make it easier for you to work out a compromise with your coworker.

5. Perspective

You can better control your emotions by putting them
into perspective by gaining a sense of perspective.
For instance, if you feel anxious before presenting a
presentation to an audience, you can put that
emotion into perspective by acknowledging that it's
common to experience some fear while speaking in
front of an audience and that many great
professionals do as well. Keeping things in
perspective will help you remember that feelings are
a normal reaction to events and that you can work
through them to complete your objectives.

Here are some methods you can utilize to improve your capacity for emotional control. Some of these methods, such as breathing exercises, might assist you in controlling your emotions when under stress or excitement. Others, like journaling, are routine activities that might help you become better at responding to people or circumstances.

1. Provide some space for your self

It can be beneficial to briefly excuse yourself when something is causing an emotional response in you. Regaining composure and exercising your reflective abilities can both be facilitated by physically removing yourself from a situation. In order to find some space, you can stroll outside or to the break room or water cooler. You can go to a window close by and peek outside if you work remotely. You may frequently return to the situation calmly and come up with a solution once you've acquired some perspective on your feelings.

2. Look for a ways to articulate your emotions

You can better control your emotions at work if you can freely express them outside of the office. You may make a phone call to friends or family and vent to them about how you're feeling. By doing so, you could also be able to gain their opinions or insight on your experiences. If you have artistic talent, you might write, draw, or paint to communicate your feelings.

3. Explore mindfulness

A meditation practice called mindfulness focuses on the feelings and sensations you are experiencing right now. Exercises in mindfulness are meant to help you focus on the here and now without worrying about the past or the future. You can find peace and perspective regarding your emotions and daily activities by practicing mindfulness. Start your meditation practice by paying attention to your breathing and the sensations in your desk chair or car for a few minutes every morning.

4. Identify what brings you joy.

Self-awareness is recognizing good feelings and the reasons behind them. By identifying the aspects of your work that make you feel good, you can develop a strong sense of accomplishment in what you do, which may make you more tenacious when facing challenges. In your office or cubicle, you could want to hang a list of the aspects of your job that you find satisfying.

5. find out techniques for breathing

While you're experiencing strong emotions, you can control your emotions by using a variety of breathing techniques. You can lessen the effect that the feeling will have on your body and thoughts by concentrating on your breathing, which may help you finish your activity or find a solution. Deeply inhale and exhale while slowing down your breathing during a breathing workout. Breathing in for four counts, holding your breath for two counts, and then exhaling for another four counts constitutes a typical breathing exercise.

6. Read books or listen to podcasts about managing your emotions.

Numerous books and podcasts provide methods to enhance emotional control, with a focus on mental health or productivity. They can also provide you with information on the brain chemistry associated with emotional responses and other details that can aid in your comprehension of your emotions. These resources are typically located in a bookstore's or online podcast provider's self-help section.

7. Keeping a mood journal will help.

Keeping a daily journal might help you better understand your emotional reactions and learn how to control them. Include details on how you felt that day and what circumstances led to various emotional reactions when you're writing in your journal. Re-reading your diary entries will help you identify your typical emotional triggers, which will help you anticipate how you will react to circumstances in the future.

8. Think about talking to a specialist

You may increase your productivity and create a healthy work life by learning effective emotional management techniques from a licensed therapist. They might conduct individual treatment sessions or guide support groups for a variety of conditions. Meeting with a therapist can provide you the freedom to express your emotions openly, learn the causes of your emotional reactions, and develop coping mechanisms in a secure environment. In order to help you even more, they can also suggest materials and activities.

CHAPTER EIGHT

Ways to overcome roadblocks of anger and fear

How to get rid of fear

I recently stumbled upon these wise words by American author Brian Andreas. Say sure, he says. Say yes with all of your heart to whatever it is. As straightforward as it may sound, this is all the motivation life requires to grasp your hands and start dancing. I believe a life that is constantly in motion might get tiresome for the majority of us realistic, cynical individuals. However, I do concur that all it takes to discover your small dose of daily happiness and the will to keep going is to be open to new experiences and challenges.

Have you been considering taking a vacation for some time but have been concerned of what it would mean for your career? Have you considered changing careers or launching a business, but the thought of stepping outside your comfort zone intimidates you? Are you avoiding taking on a new task, responsibility, or project at work out of concern that you won't succeed? These are some of the ways that fear shows up and prevents you from advancing in life and in your work. I've been there, too, and am far too conscious of my flaws to try anything new. But as time went on, I came to understand that while having a self-awareness is good, having new experiences is much better. You can get through these worries, yes.

Keep in mind that nothing spells the end of the world.

Except maybe for regret take a long view. Prioritize. Are you at ease with remembering all the opportunities you passed up one morning? Decisions will be that much simpler once you can compare your two possibilities, fear and regret.

Determine the source of your fear.

You can get some peace of mind by identifying the source of your worry. For instance, my biggest concern when I first made the decision to take a break from my full-time job was financial reliance. Once I discovered it, it was simple for me to start saving for a sabbatical fund. Whatever the difficulty, a solution can always be found. But doing so requires reflection.

Simplify

Making important life decisions might be difficult sometimes because of the complexity we have allowed ourselves to become involved in. Divide the ultimate objective up into smaller jobs. Determine the actual effects of your choice rather than what you have been taught will happen. For instance, starting your own firm or doing freelance work is likely to consume so much of your time in the beginning that you will have to give up taking that lengthy annual vacation. It hardly sounds like a trade-off on its own. But it sounds like an unduly complex, challenging trade-off when you compare it to social pressure to post the greatest vacation pics on Facebook. You should identify your own priorities and work toward them. More importantly, acknowledge the compromises and superfluous detail for what they are.

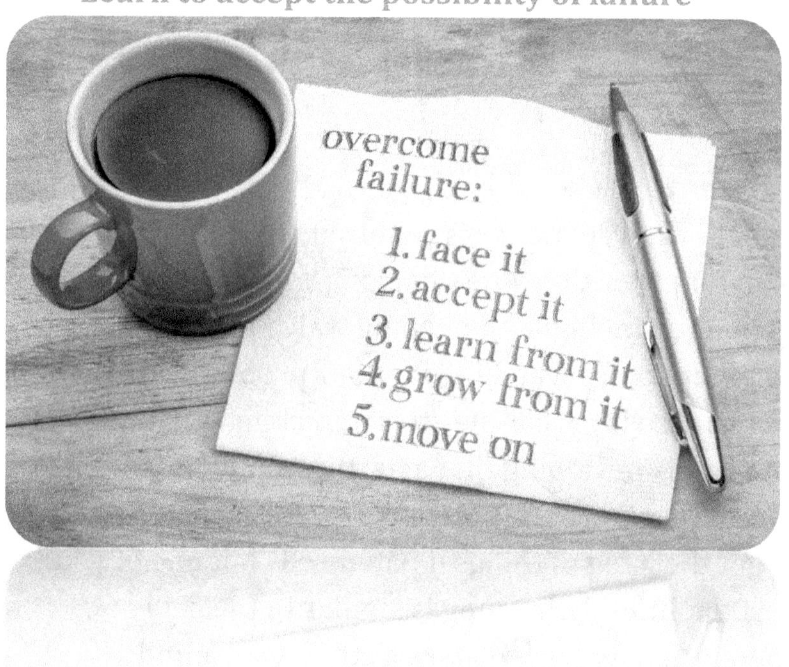

There's a good chance that your initial startup won't be a smashing success. There are many possible traps on the road to discovering your actual passion or pursuing a dream. Take a look at your what-if situations if that discourages you. Will the world truly end as we know it? little chance. You may always get a job again. Try again at the very least with much more insight into what works and what doesn't. More importantly, you won't be able to create a solid contingency plan until you learn to embrace the possibility that you might fail while trying something new for the first time.

Unbelievably, patience is required more for change than for repetition. Life-changing transformation frequently involves an ongoing waiting game, whether you're watching for your proposals to materialize into real-life stories, picking up new skills on the job, or hoping that an astute venture capitalist would recognize the potential of your idea. It's time to get the hang of things if patience is not one of your best qualities. Reframing is similar to the skill of conquering fear. It involves putting your mind through beneficial thought-training. Go for it and have some trust.

Anger

In the majority of houses, angry outbursts are frequent. When kids are quickly annoyed with one another, nasty words and behaviors frequently result. She cries, "Get out!" when Little Bobby enters his elder sister's bedroom. Two brothers are racing down the stairs when one elbows the other to gain the upper hand. They soon start pushing and yelling at one another. When Meg, the younger sister, gets left out of a game by her elder sisters, she begins to yell and strike. So, managing your anger is a key skill in the relationship curriculum.

Identify your anger

Helping kids identify anger before they explode is the first task. The amount of time between the trigger and the outburst appears to be short for some people, if not zero. But everyone of us has early indicators of when rage is about to start. Just a few indicators include hunched shoulders, tightened teeth, pursed lips, lowered eyebrows, and an agitated tone of voice. Because each person is unique, each person must be able to identify the signs of impending rage in their own bodies. To help a child develop their ability to identify anger, parents can sit down with them, discuss early warning signals, and be open about their own anger management.

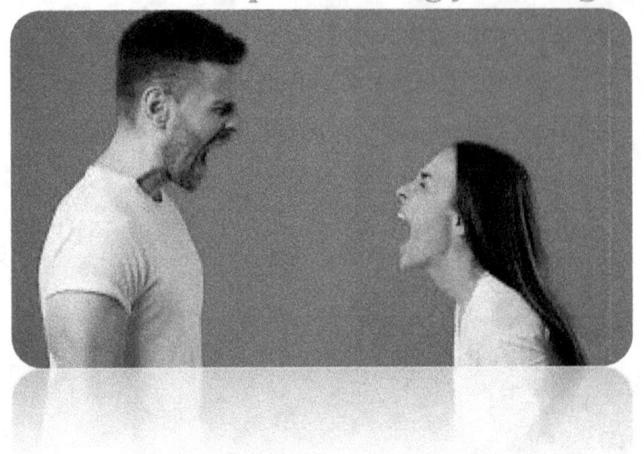

The next stage is to pause and calm down once someone anticipates becoming angry. A deep breath may be all that's required if the annoyance is only somewhat frustrating, such as when someone blocks your view of the television. The best method to stop anger may be to take a short break away from the situation if it has intensified, such as when the infant spills apple juice on some homework. Sometimes both kids and grownups lose their ability to reason when they are angry. The anger has them under control. If so, they require a bigger pause or break.

Debrief

A debriefing is necessary once the child has calmed down and taken a rest. "What did you do wrong?" is an excellent question to ask. What would you do in your own way the next time, in a non-accusatory tone, is asked. If these issues are discussed, kids will gain understanding of the problem and learn how to make the necessary adjustments.

Children need other coping mechanisms besides violent outbursts. Talking about the issue, asking for assistance, slowing down, and persevering are all positive ways to release the energy.

Even anger is a sign. It indicates that there is a problem. In some cases, the angry individual contains that something. Unrealistic expectations, for instance, can cause anger. Sometimes injustice, a violation of one's rights, or a missed opportunity is the root of rage. No of the source, anger is useful for spotting issues but not for fixing them.

Here are some other suggestions for managing anger at home:

- Never get into a debate with an angry child. Allow them to pause and continue their discussion later.

- Help kids identify anger's many guises, including bad attitudes, muttering, staring, and harsh tones of speech.
- People should acknowledge their mistakes and ask for forgiveness when their irrational words or actions harm other people.

Teach Conflict Resolution

Although kids can learn to control their rage, harmony cannot be achieved with this alone. Honor involves going above and above what is required and treating others with respect. Children need a picture of what it means to be a peacemaker rather than a troublemaker in order to get over the obstacle of anger.

Several doable suggestions for assisting kids in becoming peacemakers are provided below.

- Aim to agree rather than disagree;
- Seek out solutions that benefit all parties involved rather than those where one person benefits at the expense of others;
- Motivate yourself with love, not rage or malice.

The answer here could come from you. Find a solution that will satisfy everyone. Now, I'm eager to support and compliment them whenever I see one of them compromising or attempting to appease someone. My kids are becoming peacemakers, and while it has taken a lot of work, I am happy with the results.

A child should occasionally put up with little irritations and learn to resist being provoked. A youngster should tell an adult about an issue if they have tried to address it but it still cannot be dropped. This is not gossip. It is adhering to a conflict resolution model. If two persons are unable to solve a problem together, one of them should enlist a third party in the process.

Children develop tolerance when adults act as peacemakers. An alert system with a predetermined tolerance level is installed in people's skulls. The alert sounds when they become annoyed or irritated. The alarm is set in a unique way for each person. The levels of tolerance in children and adults differ.

It's a relief to know that tolerance thresholds can change. Children are able to modify their tolerance levels and regulate how frequently the alert sounds in their interactions with one another with a little effort. Children who are respected learn to put others' needs above their own.

Gratify advancement

When young people develop a picture of themselves as peacemakers, it is interesting to witness. They produce encouragingly original solutions. This account was given by a mother. Jenny, my daughter who is eight, adores mediating conflict. Currently, she views her fury as a chance to assist. She sees others' rage as a challenge and frequently responds, "I've got an idea..."

We were recently shopping when we noticed a
person in line in front of us becoming agitated. I have
an idea, Jenny remarked as she raised her head to
face him. While we wait, let's engage in some
enjoyable conversation. Although the man answered
and seemed to love talking with my kid, at first I felt a
little embarrassed. She had made me proud. She was
promoting peace.

CHAPTER NINE

Factors that impact your emotions

The social, mental, psychological, and spiritual facets of people's lives are included in socio-emotional health and wellbeing. This includes having and sustaining satisfying and healthy relationships, seeing things from another person's point of view, resolving interpersonal conflict, feeling competent and whole, expressing emotions, managing stress, and having a positive sense of oneself, including creating a positive sense of identity in relation to one's race and ethnicity, gender, sexual orientation, ability, disability, spirituality, and other aspects of human differences. Our potential for emotional wellbeing plays a significant role in both our social and emotional health.

The ability to manage our emotions properly, react to life's events with less reactivity and upset, and live with a feeling of meaning and purpose as we live in accordance with our basic beliefs are all examples of emotional wellness, according to Michigan State University's Employee Assistance Program. From the research of MSU emotional wellness counselors, we have compiled a list of 10 characteristics that affect emotional wellness.

Please be present right this second. Learning more about how practicing mindfulness can improve general health and wellness; spending more time in the present moment rather than thinking about the past or the future.

Understanding that our perception of life stems mostly from within us rather than from external situations or occurrences in our lives

Personal responsibility: Having an inside-out perspective on the universe enables us to assume more accountability for our emotions, ideas, and responses to the experiences of life. We can hurt fewer people—including ourselves—when we're able to recognize our own patterns of behavior and responses.

Accepting what is viewing our surroundings more objectively and recognizing what is. This involves asking ourselves, "Given that it is what it is, how do I want to respond to this situation in ways that is consistent with my values in who I wish for the world and the globe?""

Respect for the unknown: Releasing the need to be in control and possess all the information we believe is necessary to understand a situation. In order to respect the unknown, we must admit that there are many situations in life where we just cannot predict how things will turn out. I don't get to know this right now, we can tell ourselves at times.

Regaining perspective on our lives and our circumstances requires taking a step back and adopting a bigger, more universal and expanded vision of who we are.

The ability to contribute to individuals and causes that are consistent with our beliefs and that give our lives meaning and purpose comes from engaging with our communities and the greater world in ways that important to us.

Reasons Why Emotions Matter

Your thoughts and behaviors are significantly influenced by your emotions. The emotions you encounter on a daily basis can spur you to action and have an effect on both major and minor life decisions.

Emotions can be fleeting, like a flash of irritation at a coworker, or they can be persistent, like enduring sadness at the end of a relationship. But why do we actually feel emotions? What purpose do they fulfill?

From Where Do Emotions Originate?

The limbic system is the collective name for a network of linked brain regions that regulates emotions. Emotions and behavioral reactions are greatly influenced by important components such the limbic cortex, hippocampus, amygdala, and hypothalamus.

The Three Elements of emotion

It is vital to comprehend the three components of an emotion in order to properly understand it. Each component has a potential impact on the kind and intent of your emotional reactions.

- Subjective element: Your personal emotional experience
- Your body's reaction to an emotion physically
- How you respond to the emotion constitutes the expressive component.

You Can Act Due to Your Emotions

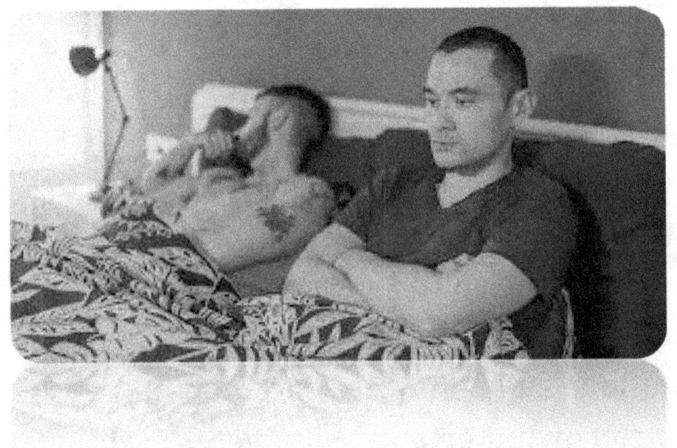

When taking a test that makes you nervous, you could experience a lot of worry about how well you'll do and how the examination will affect your final grade. You might be more motivated to learn as a result of these feelings.

You were inspired to act and do something constructive to increase your chances of receiving a good mark since you were motivated to do so because you felt a particular emotion.

You as well tend to behave in certain ways to make it more likely that you will feel joyful and less likely that you will feel unhappy. You could, for instance, look for pastimes or social activities that give you a sense of fulfillment, joy, and vigor. On the other side, you would generally steer clear of any circumstances that would cause boredom, unhappiness, or fear.

Your emotions can help you stay safe.

One of the first scientists to investigate emotions scientifically was the naturalist Charles Darwin. According to him, emotions are adaptations that help both humans and animals live and procreate.

He argued that emotional outbursts can also be crucial to life and safety. If you came across an animal that was hissing or spitting, you would immediately know that it was enraged and on the defensive, and you should move back and avoid any potential harm.

Emotions can also get the body ready to move. Particularly the amygdala is in charge of setting off emotional reactions that get your body set up to deal with emotions like fear and rage.

The fight-or-flight response, which sets off a range of physiological reactions that prime the body to either remain and face the threat or leave to safety, can occasionally be brought on by this fear.

Your ability to move fast and make decisions that will increase your chances of success and survival is one way that emotions play an adaptive function.

Your Emotions Can Influence Your Decisions

Everything you decide to do—from what to eat for breakfast to who to vote for in elections—is greatly influenced by your emotions.

Additionally, studies have revealed a lower capacity for wise decision-making in those who have particular kinds of brain injury that affect emotional sensitivity.

Emotions are a major factor in decision-making, even when you think logic and reason are the only factors at play. The ability to comprehend and control your emotions, or emotional intelligence, has been found to be crucial for making decisions.

Emotions Aid in Better Understanding by Others

When engaging with people, it's essential to leave clues so that others can understand your emotional condition. These cues may include physical manifestations of emotion, such as different facial expressions related to the specific emotions you are feeling.

In other situations, it could entail being honest about your emotions. When you share your feelings with friends or family, whether they are pleased, sad, enthusiastic, or scared, you are providing them with crucial information that they may utilize to take appropriate action.

Your ability to understand others' emotions

In the same way that your own emotions provide important information to others, the emotional expressions of others around you reveal a lot of social data. Being able to recognize and respond to other people's emotions is crucial for social communication, which plays a significant role in your daily life and relationships.

It enables you to interact with friends, family, and other loved ones in a more meaningful way and to respond accordingly. Additionally, it enables you to interact socially in a number of settings, such as

handling an unhappy client or controlling an excitable
staff.

Most Commonly Asked Questions

Where in the brain do emotions get processed?

The network of brain areas and structures that
process emotions is called the emotional processing
network. The hippocampus, prefrontal cortex,
amygdala, and cingulate cortex are among the brain
regions that are engaged in this process.

Why do emotions play a big role in decision-making?

A decision-maker can use emotions to identify the
decision-making criteria that are most pertinent to
their particular circumstance. They could facilitate
quicker decision-making as well.

The evaluation theory of emotion is what?

According to this view, people's cognitive
assessments of particular occurrences are separated
from their emotions. It suggests that people must
consider a situation before responding emotionally,
in other words.

CHAPTER TEN

How to grow by utilizing your emotions

What You Can Do To Take Advantage Of Your Emotions!

Research has produced many false assumptions due to the complexity of emotions. Emotions now have a bad reputation as a result of it. Emotions are your superpower, and you may use them to your advantage, as we learn more about them.

High achievers can be distinguished from others who are merely attempting to make it and are unable to bring about the required change by having a well-developed emotional intelligence, which is not

emotional sensitivity but rather a reflective
awareness of the complexity of emotions.

Why is it the case?

You might not be aware, but only good feelings can
bring about effective change. The reason for this is
that when we have pleasant experiences and
thoughts, our brain creates and forms new neural
pathways. Negative feelings and experiences prevent
the growth of new brain pathways, to paraphrase the
previous sentence. We are unable to learn, be
innovative, or develop answers to new issues as a
result of them.

That isn't to say you shouldn't try to make sure you're
happy. However, to fully comprehend how the
opposite side of the coin appears, the whole range of
emotions must be considered. It's possible to realize
what true joy is without having any concept of loss or
even despair.

Most certainly, you've heard the stereotypes that Latin countries are very sentimental, Americans are frequently seen as being false, and eastern European countries are quite pessimistic. Even though some of these are exaggerated, culture goes beyond customs, principles, and social conventions. It modifies how we perceive and communicate emotion. It describes the emotions we should feel and exhibit in various circumstances. Consequently, I and you will probably have different perspectives on emotions. We may even use alternative means of emotion expression.

I remember spending a birthday in Florida with my exchange-host family, to give you an example. They baked a beautiful cake, had a wonderful birthday present, and were extremely happy to see me there. They asked me if I liked the gift after I opened it, and in my characteristically German fashion, I said, "Yes, it's good." Given that I didn't express my utter delight at the present, for many Americans that suggests I didn't like it very much. I wasn't merely controlling my feelings and suppressing them. I never mastered the phrase that would have shown how much I appreciated the present in an American setting.

Various psychological and societal debates have been inspired recently by the topic on how to be emotionally sensitive. empathic traits and a greater capacity for comprehending emotion are among the themes covered. This terrain is particularly challenging to travel since many people believe that it is more vital to give yourself space to experience everything you are feeling and to pay attention to your own feelings.

First off, simply because someone feels everything doesn't automatically imply that they have strong social-emotional skills. Understanding how your emotions effect other people and putting your feelings into context are two different things from simply feeling what you are feeling. Second, how you interpret these feelings may vary. Consequently, it is simple to misread emotions. I frequently witness this when women express their enthusiasm for a project and men interpret it as being overly sentimental.

Intelligence vs. emotional sensitivity

It is vital to develop emotional intelligence, which enables a full-spectrum reflection on emotions, rather than emotional sensitivity. Therefore, it is not necessary to immediately decode the feelings of others. Instead, it is important to provide room for reflection because emotions are a complicated social construct that extends beyond the realm of physical sensation.

Three aspects of emotions

Emotions consist of three parts, as previously stated and demonstrated in my research on "masculinity and emotions in high-security prison facilities": The three E's stand for experiencing, evaluating, and expressing. Therefore, emotions are another dynamic social activity that is constantly changing. They do not adhere to fixed cultural constructions or predetermined rules. Our individual imprints on how

to comprehend our emotions are unique to everyone
of us. Our emotional world is influenced by a variety
of elements, including our social surroundings,
gender, family structure, and cultural background.

We are emotional, not rational, beings, and this is the
one thing that all humans have in common.
Therefore, our emotions have an impact on our
reasoning. We are unable to be anything other than
subjective in our relationships and judgments
without a trained reflecting process. Furthermore, I
believe that it is difficult to achieve complete
objectivity. But even so, we are able to recognize how
we are affecting our decision-making process through
an adequate reflective approach.

Why should we abandon the notion that reason is the only basis for making decisions?

A full-body experience, at the risk of sounding overly
holistic, is life. To be able to construct complete
memories, we require all of our senses. We can
perceive, hear, touch, see, and smell our
surroundings. However, many people argue that
judgments should only be made using rational
thought, which entails taking into account the past,
present, and future while making predictions. A
decision that yields results according to calculations
is successful. But things in life are always changing.

Everything around us is always changing; therefore if you behave contrary to physical principles, your forecast may rapidly become problematic.

Consider using an all-integrating method when making decisions rather than relying solely on the path of decision-making.

Decision-making from a holistic perspective

Even if the word "holistic" offends you, please stick with me for a bit. You can create decisions by using your reasoning/logic, motivation/desire, intuition, creativity, physicality/body, and emotions, which are the six pillars mentioned before.

Instead of incorporating all part of our human experience, many people prefer to make judgments and rely on one or a small number of pillars. You can't turn off your emotions, especially when the emotional aspect is often neglected or suppressed. You don't consider how your emotions are influencing your decision-making process, instead.

The economic crisis of 2008, when fear was one of the main motivating factors for many financial investors, serves as the best illustration of this (read more here). Because emotions are contagious, the severity of the scenario may have been avoided by practicing emotional control and knowledge of both individual and group emotions. Restraining your emotions won't make you more sensible. Instead, you avoid making thoughtful decisions because you are terrified of going through the entire process. Allowing yourself to go into your emotions enables you to use your decision superpower.

This justifies the status of emotional intelligence as a superpower.

The other type of intelligence is the ability to think emotionally. It entails comprehending both our own and other people's emotions. In light of this, it enables us to engage in constructive communication with one another. In particular, it will help us realize that the other person is doing the greatest effort possible. As a result, we can also:

- Cultivate wholesome connections
- Builds positive and trustworthy relationships

- You'll be able to communicate more clearly as a result.
- Be more prosperous
- And enables you to tenderly and nurturingly express your emotions
- eliminates conflict

However, there is a lot more to it. Evolution and advancement are caused by feelings of happiness.

Why stepping back and taking a deep breath can help you comprehend your feelings.

You can be more successful in life if you have the ability to sit back from your emotions and study them rather than quickly responding to them. A key step in determining where you focus your attention and how you get through challenging situations is choosing which emotions you respond to. It enables you to lessen the negative effects of stress on your body and mind. Acquiring a mindset that enables you to succeed and achieve your goals.

Resilience is increased by emphasizing good feelings and generating more happy experiences (emotional resources needed for coping). Positive feelings increase awareness, which makes it easier for us to identify more solutions to issues. Furthermore, the most recent findings in brain science provide solid evidence that pleasant emotions foster creativity and shield us from degenerative conditions like Alzheimer's, Parkinson's, and early-onset dementia.

Additionally, research demonstrates that individuals perform at their highest levels while experiencing at least three times as many good emotions as negative ones. This is because they feel better.

What steps may we take to encourage good feelings as our course of action?

How do I erase or transform my bad feelings is one of the queries I frequently get from customers. How therefore, even in the midst of my depression, can I cultivate more joyful feelings?

With the second, let's get things going. One of the common problems is the propensity of our own cultures—particularly individualistic cultures—to focus on the unfavorable remarks made by those around you. This is, of course, influenced by the negative bias to some extent, but culture also has a big impact on how we see our environment.

The second issue that many of us face is that we are always competing with one another, which results in an ongoing condition of comparison. Our self-worth is diminished and our identity is called into question by this alone.

We rely our sense of self on our feelings, which is the third challenge we are confronting. The personalization of feelings is one of the causes of such. Thus, we take every sensation we experience to be an expression of who we are personally. The capacity to sit back and evaluate your emotions objectively at this point can make a significant difference.

We should not forget that emotions are socially and culturally formed. They're designed to maintain our composure. On the other hand, certain feelings, particularly those of power and humiliation, have a permanent negative impact on how we develop personally. They are intended to embarrass you. It goes without saying that they are essential for appropriate social functioning, but they frequently create a bad impression that can quickly lead to sadness and anxiety. They also stop you from developing into your ideal self.

To counteract the propensity toward negativity and the negative societal implications, positive emotion cultivation is a crucial step. And this is the way you can go about it.

- Think about other people and how they help you. Give others your honest gratitude in particular. Focusing on others and the joy they bring into your life has been proven to be one of the most effective ways to clear your mind of negativity and negative feelings.

- Honor your talents: Recognizing your talents can help you realize that you have the ability to influence change and get through challenging circumstances.

- Keep a thankfulness diary on hand. For instance, try to list the positive things that occurred each day in the evening. When you are feeling sad, look over the journal. Clearly make an effort to concentrate on the pleasant feelings you have felt in these circumstances. Putting into words how you felt when things went well might be helpful. And think about these feelings. You can alter your perspective by changing your attention.

- Speak with someone who views the matter differently. Yes, there are moments when we need sympathy and a sympathetic ear. I firmly believe that one of the ways to pick yourself back up is to let your anger out. It's similar to cleansing your mind of unfavorable ideas. However, if it takes more than a few hours, you could require assistance to help you escape negativity and enter a condition of flexibility (set vs. flexible mindset). Make sure you have a list of individuals who can provide you with an alternative viewpoint, and be honest in your request.

- Evaluating your actions. For every claim you make, come up with a counterargument. We live in a dynamic world, and our emotional experiences are no different. Without feeling unhappy, keep in mind. Positive ones wouldn't be possible for you to have. What's required is the contrast. Therefore, when you find yourself mired in negativity, attempt to contrast your ideas and feelings.

- In a bad experience from your past, look for the good. And think back on the things that affected your life more profoundly over time.

- Make time for maintaining relationships with the individuals in your life that are important to you and giving them your time and attention.

- Send heartfelt congratulations. You can do this to both put others' needs first and establish deep relationships. And keep in mind that feelings spread easily. To put it another way, you will feel good if you make someone else feel good.

Practice of mindfulness and looking for the bright side in challenging circumstances are additional activities that support the development of good emotions. Dopamine and oxytocin levels can be raised by viewing comedies and reading humorous novels. Consequently, two hormones have a big impact on how we feel.

Another method for beginning to alter your thoughts and feelings is to see how others respond to challenging circumstances. You might also want to journal about the following issues:

- What can you learn from folks who maintained their positive outlook on life while suffering great loss?
- Have you, or anybody you know, grown as a result of suffering?

Study other cultures.

Traveling is one of my favorite and best strategies for preventing and eradicating depression and a bad life experience. And when I say travel, I don't mean taking an all-inclusive trip where you never leave your hotel or boat (though occasionally, even this can be quite productive). Particularly if you are on the verge of burnout) the traveling to nations with various cultures is what I mean. South Africa or Mozambique is two of my favorite locations. Instead of focusing on what you have and what these individuals lack in these situations, we should be inspired by how positively they are approaching life despite not having everything we possess.

How do you stay present in the moment?

You do receive regular reminders to live in the present. And indeed, a lot of books, podcasts, Clubhouse spaces, and other materials promote mindfulness and meditation. However, this is among the most difficult things to do. You can learn about and rediscover what it means to be in the moment when you travel and see how people from other cultures live their daily lives.

And one of the best ways to be able to have good feelings is to be in the present. Notably, making these memories will enable you to develop resilience.

By the way, I love to practice mindfulness while I travel.

In order to be a more effective leader or to understand how to produce more good emotions in your life, are you looking for support? Please get in touch with me, and let's explore how we can cooperate.

CHAPTER ELEVEN

How to Change and Control Your Emotions

Your degree of success and happiness are significantly influenced by your capacity to regulate and alter your emotions. Things happen extremely naturally and nearly effortlessly when you're feeling terrific, and everything seems lot easier. Right now, everything is going perfectly for you!

Taking responsibility for your emotional state is necessary for effective emotion regulation and management. It's challenging, but if you fully comprehend what sets off your emotions, you'll be able to control how you react when life gives you a curveball.

I'll go through nine particular strategies in this article that you may use right away to change and manage your emotions. I'm confident that things will start to

change in your life if you apply these exact strategies
and mindset adjustments. Your life will begin to
reflect more positive emotions like joy, happiness,
fulfillment, and love, and your general mental health
will significantly improve.

Most individuals think that emotions function in this
way. You may feel happy or unhappy after an
incident. For instance, you may receive a fantastic
new job and be eager to begin. You feel pleased when
you receive praise for work that you have done well.
You're anticipating your vacation and you're excited.
You feel happy when your partner or a friend shows
kindness toward you.

The reverse is also true. Your work is criticized by a
demanding supervisor, making you feel
unsatisfactory. After your vacation, you go through
"post-holiday blues." You experience anxiety due to a
financial hardship or frustration over a physical
ailment.

The issue with this method of thinking is that it assumes that your mental state is dependent on external factors. You've got no power over it. Furthermore, it's a concern because emotions influence behavior. You're much more likely to work harder and accomplish more when you're energized, motivated, joyful, and confident. You are more inclined to put off doing something or say something you regret later when you are angry, upset, sad, or annoyed.

Therefore, most people think that their capacity for action is influenced by how they feel. The way people feel is influenced by outside circumstances or life events, which are partially out of your control Situations and occurrences in life are subject to our control, but not entirely however, you have power over how you interpret and respond to outside circumstances.

Exactly how emotions operate

This is the actual procedure! A circumstance or life experience happens, sparking a thought about it. This idea therefore gives that circumstance some meaning. Depending on a belief you hold, that meaning may change. The belief will frequently be based on a prior encounter. This causes a feeling, which causes a behavior or action, which causes a result. Depending on how you feel about the outcome, a new feeling is created.

The situations or events in our lives that we think about influence how we feel and behave. However, because it all occurs so quickly and is completely unconscious, most people don't see it in this way.

This is illustrated in the following example. The same business dismisses two employees. I'll never get another job, the first individual thinks. The underlying conviction that "I'm not good enough" may support this, which causes the person to feel depressed, angry, resentful, or disappointed. In addition to the main conviction that "I'm not good enough," he may also think other things, such as "I'm awful at interviews" or "I'm too old to find another project these also bring on additional negative feelings.

After being laid off, the second individual may think, "I have wonderful abilities and experience," "I did a really good job there," "It's time for a change anyhow," or "I can obtain a job with higher money." Behind all of these ideas is the fundamental conviction that "I am good enough." This person consequently experiences good feelings like assurance, acceptance, or even exhilaration. This will encourage him to look for employment elsewhere or maybe launch his own company.

Therefore, rather than the actual incident, it is your interpretation of the scenario or life event that causes your thoughts and subsequent feelings. Being laid off means nothing in and of itself you unintentionally give it a meaning, and each person's meaning is unique.

People tend to simply give situations one meaning, which is another mistake. Numerous interpretations or meanings are possible. What else could this signify, ask yourself? The interpretation you give to this determines its sole meaning, so keep that in mind.

It's time to learn how to stop situations and emotions from acting as automatic triggers. This may require some effort, patience, and tenacity because it is so unconscious and natural, but trust me, the effort will be worthwhile. Here are some fantastic strategies to help you manage and modify your emotions.

Awareness

Everything begins with becoming aware. Understand that you can manage your emotions. Remember that you are the one who gives a circumstance thought—its meaning. An emotion is produced by the thinking (and the belief it is based on). You act (or don't act) on this emotion, which then triggers other thoughts and feelings that appear to rely on how the action turns out.

You will begin to recognize yourself when negative situations occur as your awareness grows. By thinking of fresh ideas and giving the circumstance new meaning, you can break the cycle. Watch your emotions to see how they alter.

It's best to catch yourself as soon as possible. Blood moves from the prefrontal cortex (the rational, reasoning portion of your brain) to the amygdala when the unpleasant feeling intensifies (the emotional brain). This explains why it's challenging to think clearly when you're anxious or upset.

If you don't catch yourself in time, wait until the feelings subside and then consider another way to approach the situation. What constructive interpretations and meanings may I give to this circumstance?

Your emotional wellness depends on your ability to take full responsibility for your feelings.

When to allow yourself to feel bad

Major life events necessitate a grieving or adjustment phase. These might consist of.

- Loss of a close relative
- Breakup of a relationship
- Redundancy

Significant health issue or concern taking the time to fully express all the sadness and other feelings you have had as a result of this significant life event is a part of the mourning process. To go through this significant life shift, you will probably need the assistance of a close friend or even a counselor.

Take advantage of this time to evaluate your life and possibly make some changes. Your best life-altering choices may occasionally occur in the most hopeless circumstances.

Acceptance is the end result of the grieving process. Take your time with this; don't be hard on yourself.

Put Negative Emotions to Rest

Many people store their feelings inside or suppress them when it comes to dealing with them. As it adds more tension, this could be harmful to your health. Additionally, since these feelings are too strong to be kept inside forever, your unconscious mind will try to let them out. This explains why some people become agitated over seemingly unimportant issues. This is comparable to the straw that broke the camel's back.

The other option is to voice your feelings. This is beneficial for you, but it's not so beneficial if you frequently communicate your emotions to a spouse or close friend. When this happens, a qualified therapist can assist you in expressing and then permanently releasing your emotions.

Release of emotions is the third alternative, which the majority of people are unaware of. The Sedona Method is my go-to technique for letting go of my emotions. The Emotional Freedom Technique (EFT) and hypnotherapy are both excellent alternatives.

This is an excellent practice to teach you how to manage and modify your emotions. It entails increasing your awareness of your emotions and the things that appear to set them off. Throughout the next week, pay closer attention to your negative emotions. Consider pausing to assess your feelings. Recognize and record the thoughts that underlie the emotion. What kind of ideas am I currently having?

Here, it's important to keep feeling the bad emotions. Instead, you start to become aware of the thoughts and record them. You won't catch them all, but

You'll catch enough of them to see the connection between your feelings and the underlying concepts.

Asking questions can alter the meaning.
By asking yourself questions like these, you can alter the meaning of these thoughts.

- What makes this good?
- What further might this imply?

Asking the proper questions drives your mind to look for the positive aspects of a circumstance or occurrence. Finding the good may need some persistence at times, but it can always be found if you look for it and ask the appropriate questions.

Adjust your focus

Similar to shifting the meaning, this focuses more on your constant thoughts and your perceptions of the circumstance. Start concentrating more on what you want in the redundancy example. For example, you might picture yourself acing interviews, visualize a wealth of prospects, or remind yourself of all the excellent abilities and experience you currently possess. Focusing on what you desire requires more time and emotional effort.

Physiological changes

Your body and emotions are extremely closely related. Your head will likely be lowered, your shoulders will likely be forward, you won't be grinning, and your breathing will likely be short if you're experiencing unpleasant emotions.

Do the opposite consciously as soon as you realize this. Observe how the feeling or emotion changes by raising your head, grinning, taking a deep breath, and moving your shoulders back. Consider the physiology of a confident person if you wish to feel confident. They will appear at ease, smile, have their heads up, speak effectively, use gestures, and project a calm demeanor.

Your emotions will change when your physiology does, which will cause your thoughts to follow suit. When you take action, your thoughts will come afterwards.

Modify your language.

Your thoughts and words have a big impact on how you feel, both inside and externally.

Start with putting the phrase "I can't" out of your vocabulary, and then endeavor to interact with others as positively as you can. Your unconscious mind hears statements such, "I'm not very confident," or "I'm not good at interviews." Similar to a negative affirmation, it Your unconscious mind still hears what you are saying even though you are speaking to someone else.

Consistent use of positive affirmations will start to alter your emotional state—not just when you say them, but also at other times. Here are two excellent affirmations to use right away to elevate your emotional state:

- I am currently in control of my feelings.
- My emotions are under my control.

So there you have it—nine fantastic techniques to manage and alter your emotions right now and gradually increase the number of happy, unplanned emotions you experience. As I have said, situations that elicit negative emotions are frequently the result of very quick and unconscious thinking. Therefore, it will take time to create these new patterns, and consistency is key.

Having a morning habit is one of the finest methods to constantly manage and alter your emotions. You can do this or other actions first thing in the morning to rewire your brain for success. I wholeheartedly endorse a course called Morning Ritual Mastery to assist you in developing a potent morning routine that will enable you to instantly alter your emotions. I've used this method multiple times to establish powerful morning routines in my life that help me prepare myself for success each day.

Please spread the word about this post on social media or with others if you liked it and found it useful. Post your thoughts or queries in the space provided below. I'd be really interested in your opinions. Please rate this content by clicking on one of the stars below.

Ever questioned what the most prosperous people do? Who are the people who are actually content, joyful, and prosperous? So I share this in my eBook, 10 Strategies for Your Success.